Evan Eisenberg
Drawings by Steve Brodner

THE
TRUMPIAD

Terra Nova Press
NEWARK   CALLICOON   MATSALU

2019

ISBN: 978-1-949597-03-5

Published by

Terra Nova Press
NEWARK   CALLICOON   MATSALU

set in Gotham, Modern No. 20 and Giovanni
designed by Martin Pedanik
printed by Tallinn Book Printers, Tallinn, Estonia
on Munken Polar paper, flexibound

Library of Congress Control Number: 2018957965

1 2 3 4 5 6 7 8 9 10

www.terranovapress.com

Distributed by the MIT Press, Cambridge, Massachusetts
and London, England

To the Resistance

PREFACE

Before TV came along, the role of late-night comedy—to mash the pie of truth into the face of power—was played by satire in verse, often abetted by the artist's pen. Inspired by Swift, Pope, Byron, and Heine as well as by Hogarth, Gillray, Goya, and Daumier (and well aware that, as Steve put it, we are not fit to fill those boys' inkwells), we have tried to reinvent this grand tradition for our demented times.

Book One of the *Trumpiad*, which traces Trump's career from the murk of his ancestry to the muck of the 2016 campaign, was posted online (just words, no pictures) shortly before the election. Trump won anyway. Weeks later, as I inched out from under my bed, I realized that the poem, far from having been rendered irrelevant, must now accept its new role as ongoing (and, initially, online) chronicle of the Trump Maladministration in all its appalling glory.

Calculating that each of my words was worth one millipicture, I began casting about for an artist. My first stop was the legendary Edward Sorel, who loved the poem but said he'd just started work on another book. He directed me to Steve Brodner, "the best caricaturist around." It may have been the best advice I ever got.

This is fact-based art. My sources include
books and articles by writers mentioned in the
acknowledgments, as well as news clips and
reports in such notorious Fake News outlets as the
New York Times and the *Washington Post.* I have, of
course, reserved the right to make use of my hard-
earned poetic and comic license.

A word about my stanza form. I find it hard to
believe I could have invented it. More likely it
was the product of a wild night shared by Emily
Dickinson and Edward Lear.

As Book Two is the diary of a debacle, each stanza
knows only what it can see from its own perch in
time. Book Two ends as Book One did: peering
anxiously at an election that is just around the
corner and, as such, invisible. Even more anxiously,
this time. You, Sir or Madam, have the advantage
of me: you know, as you read these words, whether
democracy in America still has a fighting chance.

—E.E.
November 2018

BOOK ONE

Muse, you're fired. It's sad. Sad!
    I mean, you're a nice piece of ass—
But I can do this myself. You've heard
How smart I am? How I have the best words?
    How I was first in my class?

A man and his money I sing, O Muse—
    Muse, you heard me! Get out!
That desk had better be clear by three—
As I was saying, my theme will be
    A man, his money, his mouth.

This is the ballad of Donald Trump,
    A tale of greed and gall;
A tragedy birthed before our eyes—
A man, his money, his mouth, his rise
    And if there's a God, his fall.

A man, his money, his mouth, his rise,
    His fall—or, otherwise, ours:
If you doubt his swagger, bluster and blunders
Can lead to disaster, you're rashly misunder-
    Estimating his powers.

His tongue is fleet as Achilles' feet,
    If slightly more prone to stumble;
His wiles would make Odysseus blush,
And like Aeneas (that's Latin for "tush")
    He's always ready to rumble.

Having established his *bona fides*
    As hero, let's give his Begats,
Beginning in Kallstadt, where, by God,
The Trumps, once Drumpfs, grumpily trod
    The blood of grapes in vats.

Friedrich Trump prefigured his
    Descendant, fore and aft;
But as his feet were bone-spur-free
He had to sail across the sea
    To dodge his nation's draft.

An immigrant! An enterprising,
    Civic-minded fellow—
Thanks to whom the gold-drunk Yukon
Had a gilded floor to puke on
    In a posh bordello.

Did Dudley do right when the Mounties
 Shut that cat-house down?
Right or wrong, Trump cashed his chips,
Checked the list of east-bound ships,
 And skipped for his hometown.

He wed, and launched the burgher's life
 His frosty hoard afforded;
But Ach!—the draft board checks again,
And like a wetback Mexican
 Poor Friedrich is deported.

Chastened by King, he hastened to Queens—
     Scene of son Fred's future capers.
Blood-and-iron-willed, hungry, lean,
Fred launched his empire at sixteen
     With Mother signing the papers.

Like Friedrich, Fred was gifted with
     An instinct for what works:
Parking garages for new-fangled wheels;
New-fangled self-service grocery deals
     That let him cashier the clerks.

Fred's latest, greatest stratagem
     Was simple: he'd invite
Manhattan's huddled, muddled masses
To a paradise where grass is
     Green, and skin is white.

Where once were forests of oak and pine,
     Where once were fields and furrows,
Trump's rickety "Dumps on Stumps"
Spread like chicken pox or mumps
     Across the outer boroughs.

When G.I. Joes came marching home
     He built them seaside flats:
Noble work, nobly rewarded
With the subsidies all hoarded
     In his Homburg hat.

Such profiteering struck even
     Even-tempered Ike as rank;
Called before a Senate hearing,
Fred purred: *It isn't profiteering
     If the profit just sits in the bank!*

Enough Begats, now! Faith and begad,
     We'll strain the straps of mirth
If, lacking Tristram's comic clout,
We wear our reader's patience out
     Before our hero's birth.

His birth—*but wait!* If climate change
     Is merely a hoax hatched in China,
How do we know the Donald's not
An Erdoganic despot-bot
     Devised in Asia Minor

And engineered by Vladimir's
    Rechristened K.G.B.—
Which China will shortly mass produce—
A handy source of mass abuse
    For all humanity?

We don't. But let's be gracious and
    Concede he was conceived
By Fred on his Mary, née MacLeod,
A Scottish housemaid, broke but unbowed,
    At Ellis Isle received.

(An immigrant! Another one!
    To this surmise I'm leaping:
Should Trump meet such a one tonight
And should her skin be not-quite-white,
    He'd call her Miss Housekeeping.)

What crèche can conjure up the kings
    Who 'round the cradle stand?
Did Dolf and Benny bow to her?
And did the frankincense and myrrh
    Already bear His brand?

From youth, our *Cheeto Jesus* was
    Entirely without sin:
How else withstand a toddler's moans
While bravely showering with stones
    The crib that it was in?

(Where's that toddler, now? Does he,
    Still trumpatized, thumb-suck?
Is the memory sharp or fuzzy?
Does he watch the news, and does he,
    Seeing Donald, duck?)

More deeds served to demonstrate
    That Donald was no wuss:
Attempting to defenestrate
A chum; socking a second-grade
    School teacher in the puss.

(That last, Don's boast—the victim never
    Validated it;
But murmured to his kindred, when
Upon his deathbed, "Even then
    He was a little sh*t.")

Faced with a strapping lad intent
    On scrapping every rule,
Father Fred, severe but fair,
Remanded Donald to the care
    Of a military school.

(That window flap in fact belongs
    At this point in the plot;
But time, we know, is an illusion;
Rhyme, though in the worst confusion
    Hudibrastic, not.)

Bully to *Leader*—context shapes
    The words, and hence the man.
A hero in the making? Hell
No! His Captain's bars look too swell
    To soil them in Khe Sanh.

Three school deferments from the draft,
    And one more for good measure,
Because a well-paid doctor, Sir,
Has kindly found a fine bone spur.
    Which foot? Well, what's your pleasure?

Survivor guilt's a bitch; but Don,
    That Fury to appease,
Endured a "personal Vietnam"
By braving (*wham, bam, at ease Ma'am*)
    Venereal disease.

Thirsty, he imbibed the business
    At his father's feet:
A ton of brass, a dash of knuckle,
Plus a long, hard, steady suckle
    At the public teat.

Soon he found a second father
    To perfect his parts—
His guru (not the least Siddharthy)
None but Senator McCarthy's
    Master of Dark Arts.

Roy Cohn! The consigliere,
    Cold collusions ever hatching,
Teaches Donald how to cozy
Up to handy mafiosi
    When a back needs scratching.

Roy Cohn! The cognoscente
    Of the con, the squeeze, the steal,
The secret blade, the tidied gore,
The set-up, shakedown, flimflam, or—
    As Don would say—the Deal.

When Fred handed Donald the company's reins,
    Roy was enlisted, not for
Legal matters dry and humdrum,
But for an unreal-estate conundrum
    That would have baffled Bohr.

Is light a particle or wave?
    Depends on how it's detected.
Does Trump have vacancies right now?
Depends, in a quantumy way, on how
    The questioner's complected.

More plainly: people of color found
    Reception rather rude.
Twenty years earlier, wroth at this wrong,
Woody Guthrie wrote a song;
    Now steely Justice sued.

Countersue! cried Donald. Roy
     Rogered: *Defamation!*
Dismissed! snapped the judge, which must have nettled:
Trump, who *never settles,* settled
     For corporate probation.

Before Trump Tower could rise, Bonwit
     Teller had to fall;
For this, undocumented Poles—
Hard-hatless, maskless, homeless, cold—
     Were at Trump's beck and call.

The "Polish Brigade," when paid at all,
     Was paid the merest pittance;
Safety inspectors and union crews
At a nod from Roy Cohn, knew
     Not to seek admittance.

Two Deco nymphs were smashed to bits
     Despite their fervent suitors;
Yet we must count their fate deserved,
For surely they'd have been preserved
     Had they had bigger hooters.

While LeFraks and Resnicks all deplored
    The local mob's monopoly
Of concrete, and used steel instead,
Don with Fat Tony hopped in bed
    And did so very hoppily.

The Roman who first mixed concrete
    Now in Elysium gloats:
Behold its metamorphic powers!
For pals like Donald, topless towers;
    For others, overcoats.

Only in America
    Could such a tale unfold:
By the bootstraps that he hitches to,
Donald lifts himself from riches to
    Riches, gold to gold.

In fact, had he invested Fred's
    Multimillions in a
Nice NYSE index fund, his wad
Would be (though fans might find this odd)
    Thicker now, not thinner.

Trump's gift for turning gold to ___
    (Insert terms that disgust us):
For this our best lexicographers lack words,
But *Sadim Touch* (that's *Midas* backwards)
    Might just do it justice.

Here's a striking instance of
    An ill-advised *Trumpkrieg:*
The time he sued the N.F.L.,
Hail-Marla-passing straight to hell
    A promising young league.

The owners trusted Trump to win
    His antitrust lawsuit;
But hey, we know the system sucks—
The court awarded them three bucks.
    The U.S.F.L.? Kaput.

(Suppose it were the U.S., not
    U.S.F.L. he led?
Gambling's fun when on vacation;
Gambling when the stake's a nation—
    Darker shades of red.)

The Trump Shuttle; the grand hotel
    Eloise absolutely adored—
Though the Donald's flops are legion
The floppiest flopped in the region
    Of the Jersey shore.

The Casino Control Commission, keen
    Its Garden State to keep
Free of thugs like Bugsy Siegel
Set up eighteen months of legal
    Hoops through which to leap.

Make it six months, Trump insisted.
    Hoops? He walked around them.
Stains on ties from wise-guy vinos?
Those who licensed his casinos
    Somehow never found them.

Hilton? Denied. Attorney tied,
    It seems, to shady party.
Commishs conveniently forget
One Cohn, Esquire, whose phone is set
    On speed-dial to John Gotti.

At Trump's casinos, chopper flights
    Were furnished by a thug:
Joey Weichselbaum, whose varlets
Used a network of used car lots
    As fronts for dealing drugs.

Quite a dicey choice on Don's part!
    Might we then surmise
That Weichselbaum, besides the choppers,
Gave elite casino-hoppers
    Other kinds of highs?

When Joe went down, Don's cronies found
    A way to hide the stench:
Sentence in Jersey, where the Very
Honorable M. Trump Berry
    Occupied the bench.

Though Sis recused herself, it's clear
    Her colleagues got the brief:
*Treat our chopper guy with kid
Gloves.* So, demonstrably, they did;
    For while each petty thief

Caught up in Joey's escapade
    Got ten years, if an hour,
The mastermind got only three
And after eighteen months was free
    And living in Trump Tower.

Trump's letter asking leniency
    Might have helped (you think?) —
And might have cost his gaming license
Had not Enforcement, with its wry sense
    Humorous, merely winked.

Trump Plaza, Castle, Taj Mahal—
    As cash engorged his kitty,
The boardwalk groaned beneath the weight
Of monsters that, in due course, ate
    Each other, then the city.

Contractors, vendors, lenders, staff
    Were stiffed—lost shirts—lost skin—
But Trump emerged (*triumphant pose*)
Smelling, if not like a rose,
    Then like a Benjamin.

Though certain indexed pages *(Trump,*
    Donald, 97)
Are all he generally deigns to look
At in any given book,
    He loves Chapter Eleven.

Bankruptcy! Lifeboat that lets
    Captain Trump float free
While backers, passengers and crew of
Each of his titanic screw-ups
    Sink beneath the sea.

Cash-strapped, he now takes public his
     Casino company.
Who needs fiscal sonograms
When the ticker's monogrammed
     Like golf towels, *DJT?*

Trump chips off fifty million bucks
     In salary and bonuses;
The bough will break, the stock will fall,
Investors lose their little all:
     On them, alas, the onus is.

(A sucker, so Barnum says, is born
     Every minute, and this makes sense;
A life cycle so lively—it turns on a dime—
Allows one very little time
     To learn from experience.)

Now a fresh hope bobs like flotsam
     On the subsiding sea
Of his slots-and-roulette-wheel typhoon:
If he can't be a real tycoon,
     He'll play one on TV!

Reality TV, no less—
    That moron's oxymoron—
Where mini-Dons brave Donald's ire
Just for a shot at being hired
    As Saruman to his Sauron.

As his hot mic attested, to
    Hot chicks he makes a beeline;
The Donald needs no roll-call vote
To let his tongue patrol their throats
    Or grab them by the *feline*.

(My preference is to euphemize,
    But if you think it wussy
To beat around the Billy Bush
And primly cite *derrière* or *tush*—
    Go for it! I'm not fussy.)

Miss Universe, USA, Teen USA—
    All furnish more occasions
For fingering the ripening fruit
(He's the boss, so best be mute!)
    And dressing-room invasions.

Trump's business model now is just
     Ghost-writing gone berserk:
Flush with the spectral coins of fame
He's richly paid to put his name
     On other people's work.

Wine and water, steaks and neckties,
     Condos and cologne;
And capping the buffoonery
A real-estate tycoonery—
     A Wharton of his own!

Trump U., in truth, is not a U-
     Niversity at all;
And though he claimed the faculty
Were, to a man, "handpicked by me"
     His hands, you know, are small.

Were you among the thousands fleeced
     (Snowed, swindled, chiseled, scammed)
By "experts" hired off the street
To pressure-sell the Gold Elite
     Package for thirty grand?

Take my advice, and you may find
    Trump's lessons more endearing:
Ignore the content, mark the form!
Thus clever sheep, while being shorn
    May learn the art of shearing.

Each Trump resort must proudly sport
    Its Star Diamond Award.
The judges? Trump's family, Trump's staff,
Trump and Trump's butler, too (don't laugh),
    Who constitute the board.

The president's Joey No Socks,
 A.k.a. the Preppy Don:
Convicted felon, pusher, fence,
As acquiescent as Mike Pence
 In Donald's every con.

The Trump Foundation—there's another
 Scam, and it's a honey:
With gold-embossed pomposity
He play-acts generosity
 With other people's money.

Now Donald finds a novel use
    For his foundation's cash:
Dispensing it like Benadryl
To state Attorneys General
    Who might do something rash.

Tim Tebow's helmet, too, he scores
    With philanthropic pelf,
Plus a king-size portrait of his love—
His life, his joy, his turtle dove—
    His deity: Himself.

(Its whereabouts are now unknown.
    Did it displease der Führer?
Did it reveal that—shades of Gray!—
As he grew richer, day by day,
    His soul grew ever poorer?)

Pro among con-men, his resumé
    Still lacked one final rip-off:
Make the people he'd been screwing
Stamp and cheer for their undoing.
    Peeps, observe the tip-off:

Trump descending Trump Tower's mirrored
    Escalator, miming
The prolapse of democracy
To marble-wombed plutocracy
    With perfect comic timing.

Global capital unbound—
    'Twixt rich and poor, a chasm—
Party of the late white male
Thrashing like a great white whale
    In its final spasm—

Plotting to suppress the vote
    Of blacks and browns and youth,
Brashly gerrymandering
And very rashly pandering
    To paranoid untruth—

Other party, partly bothered
    By its own collusion
In despoiling of the earth, yet
Partly feels the spoils are worth it—
    Hence, its lame confusion—

Whirling like a centrifuge
  The nation segregates—
Inside red and outside blue—
This side's false is that side's true—
  Vanished, the debates

Where facts were facts and logic was
  Just normally impaired—
Now on social media
Whichever lie is seedier
  Is seeded, tweeted, shared—

Trump invented none of this.
    What *did* he do? Abet
All that's most foul, unfair, and fake,
And from the pot of plunder take
    Whatever he could get.

Stubby hands still greasy, now
    To clean things up he'll pledge;
From the stump and from his Twitter
Spews a manic stream of bitter
    Bile that sets on edge

Mexicans, veterans, Muslims and blacks,
    Asians and Jews and Aleutians,
Vagino-Americans of every hue,
Handicapped folks and, presumably, you
    If you've read the Constitution.

Yet white blue-collars, nest eggs paltry,
    Feathers plucked by fate,
Schooled by Fox News and hard knocks,
Rapturously back the fox
    To make the henhouse great.

Such, at least, appears to be
    The liberal CW—
Trump, like Sanders, taps the rage
Of castoffs from globalization's stage.
    True, but this fact may trouble you:

Trumpsters earn more than the national mean.
    Take the E.P.A.-noncompliant
Mortarboardless contractor whose price
Contracts as in an iron vise
    His liberal-arts-grad client—

His beef with our Bollyhued McWorld
    Is hardly economic;
But the promise to restore again
The dominance of straight white men
    Braces him like a tonic.

Foxy Trump on his barnyard stump
    Warms his inmost cockles
When he tasks that alien resident,
The Kenyan, Muslim "President,"
    With the Texas Twit's debacles.

Or blames an overbearing dame
    For—well, take your pick:
When daily for a quarter century
Your target's tarred, eventually
    Most anything will stick.

Grand Old Partyers gape as each
    Caparisoned champion's mown
Down. A clown with painted mane
Gleefully reaps the hurricane
    They themselves have sown.

Toppled are trees in whose lees
    Politicos crouched and cowered;
Uprooted rocks, the muck vacating,
Bare the pallid, pullulating
    Maggots of white power.

(Hill's LOVE TRUMPS HATE signs—what a shame
    To truck them to the dump—
Let's thwart that ecotastrophy
By adding an apostrophe
    And selling them to Trump!)

Evangelicals, you divine,
    Must shun as a pariah
This lying, grasping, adulterous fraud?
Behold! The preachers and ministers laud
    Trump as their new Messiah.

Pray, what do these good Christian folk
    And Donald have in common?
(*Scratches head.*) No clue. Unless—
Perhaps—their gospel is Success,
    Their god almighty Mammon.

Of course, there's the sort who cry "The court!"—
    Who wield love like a knife—
Reverencing every human
Till he rashly leaves the womb and
    Starts a human life.

Trump's running mate, a cunningly carved
    Etiolated tuber,
The evangelicals will wow:
He's holier than I, than Thou,
    Than Martin Freaking Buber.

Ivanka's knack for marketing
    This veep pick will confirm,
Affording swing-state ditherers
A smorgasbord of slitherers—
    The serpent and the worm.

In Pence's mouth won't melt one pat
    Of butter from your pantry;
Though they may seem like night and day,
Mike and Donald are just two ways
    Of casting Elmer Gantry.

The platform of the G.O.P.—
    A great, big, bloody bone
Thrown to those who salivate
To found a Christian caliphate
    In our once-temperate zone.

Our thrice-wed metrosexual?
    Such details merely bore him.
Let the wonks wank with planks and stuff
Just so that platform's tall enough
    For all eyes to adore him!

But hold—his people did find *some*
    Provisions worth disputing:
Precisely those that might offend
His Great-Dictator-Mentor and
    Man-Crush, Volodya Putin.

The D.N.C. hack's one big scoop?
    Believe me, this is HUGE—
The flag-draped, gold-domed candidate
Who bragged he'd MAKE AMERICA GREAT
    Is just a Russian stooge.

Tangled up with oligarchs,
　　He'll wangle them a thaw,
And, as in Putin's gangster state,
By all means needful obviate
　　The pesky rule of law.

But who will hack Trump's tax returns?
　　Not apparatchiks, surely;
Release them, just like everyone?
Of course, soon as the audit's done!
　　Donald responds demurely.

And truth to tell, this morbid interest in
    Every blessed penny
Paid by Trump at each quarter's finish
Seems a tad angels-dancing-on-pinnish
    When he pays hardly any.

Is Trump worth what he says he is?
    It's hard to know the facts
When assets are valued (this is ripe)
Fifty times more when being hyped
    Than when they're being taxed.

His net worth has no fixed abode:
    No floor, no walls, no ceiling;
And (what seems rather rad to me)
Like parts of his anatomy
    It varies with his feelings.

Is Trump a multithousandaire
    Or is it multibillions?
Such doubts would not predominate
If we could just denominate
    His net worth in *Trumpillions*.

He struts and frets the national stage
    While all the world observes:
There he blows, in spate again!
He'll make America grate again
    On all the world's nerves.

The mogul who, as cameras roll,
    All-powerful, growls "You're fired"—
To banish our despondency
Will wave his tiny wand and see
    Twenty-five million hired.

"Fingers short, nose long"—so taunt
　　His truth-obsessed accusers;
Truly, Donald's far too smart
To blurt the words that gird his heart:
　　Truth? Truth is for losers!

The sunset tints of cheek and jowl
　　That in his fans inspire
Daydreams of riches, glitz, romance,
Are but the mirrored glow of pants
　　Perpetually on fire.

"He speaks his mind." Let me remind
　　Those flummoxed by that phantom—
His mind's a jumble of paste pearls
Whose correspondence to the world
　　Is somewhat less than random.

Effete epistemologists
　　Can bitch and moan and sob.
Total losers! Lightweights! Fools!
The wise man knows that words are tools
　　You use to do a job.

48

In fact, it isn't jewels, it's tools
    That pack his cabinet mental:
File, pick, chisel, slim jim, axe—
Any relationship to facts
    Is purely accidental.

But as Trump's tools tend to be blunt
    Or jagged, or uncouth,
"He speaks his mind!" cry those who take
Civility for something fake
    And boorishness for truth.

The press was his oyster, but now they're all crabs—
    Those fact-checkers—*too* picky, *too* nitty!
They're missing the lesson he's trying to teach:
What's the point of "freedom of speech"
    If a guy can't lie with impunity?

The press that inflated him now he berates
    For detumescent polls.
Want a metaphor for that?
The man who, when it has a flat,
    Molotovs his Rolls.

The vote is rigged! Trump bellows—prim
    Republicans tut-tutting
Know well the fuming lies he fans
Were lit to justify their plans
    For Voting-Rights-Act-gutting.

It's rigged, it's rigged, it's rigged, he chants.
    The hypnotizing rhythm
Charms and arms a thronging snake—
If Donald has to lose, he'll take
    Democracy down with him.

Steaming, scattershot manure
    Prepares a bed most fecund
For mayhem and bloodshed to grow—
The only law the lawless know
    Being Amendment Second.

And that's one of the *good* outcomes.
　　Appreciably less fun:
The one where Donald and his cult
Accept, as promised, the result
　　Because… because… *he's won.*

To take the edge off edginess
　　I'll venture to repeat
Some armchair psychoanalysis
(Excluding size of phalluses)
　　While on the edge of my seat:

From paradise to barracks—did
　　Young Donald's cold rejection
By Fred the Father plant the seed
Of raging, caged-in, stage-struck need
　　And violent insurrection?

The child within the man is fathered
　　By another child,
And so (I see Tom Eliot grinning)
A spore cast at the world's beginning
　　May contain… *its end.*

But here's a cheerful thought—in fact,
    I think it's rather grand—
As the Body Pol he's screwing,
Trump's Great Dictator turn is doing
    Wonders for his brand.

(Why not license other names
    In ways likewise relentless?
Stalin Steaks! Benito's Floss!
Hitler Health Resorts! The pos-
    Sibilities are endless.)

If there's a God, his fall, I said;
    But should old Zeus or Gaea
Have lost their fulminating clout
It falls to us to bring about
    This fine peripeteia:

Of horse an ass, of jokes a butt,
    Of loserness a lump:
The king of debt, and hype, and sex—
The man who would be our T. Rex—
    Becomes, at last, T. Rump.

BOOK TWO

Muse, we are not amused. Divine
    Afflatus is all very well;
But now that Clio's colic's got us
A flatulent, fraudulent fool for a POTUS
    We're none too enthused with the smell.

College is unaffordable?
    To Bernie I cry *"D'accord!"*
Then, tapping him on the pectorals,
Append: "And the electoral's
    The one we can least afford!"

Hillary wins by three million votes;
    Trump's eighty thousand unseat her.
A better way there's gotta be—
Zounds! Methinks a lottery
    Would yield a sounder leader.

She took the high road and he took the low—
    Abysmal, abyssal, infernal;
And who do you think got to Washington first,
Flanked by the skank of America's worst,
    Red-eyed, predatory, nocturnal?

Mourning in America!
    Rosy-fingered Dawn
(Her perquisites infringed upon)
Yields to stubby-fingered Don
    To gild the White House lawn.

Inchoate hymns to Old Hickory
    Confirm our dampest fears:
Four years are—well, four years too long
For a tribe three hundred million strong
    To walk a trail of tears.

Will naked greed drive policy,
    Or loincloth'd hate and fear?
Enquiring minds that wish to know
Must ask of Trump, as of Van Gogh:
    Who has got his ear?

Here's the puzzle—ears are plural—
    Twinned, like Castor and Pollux;
If one's in Javanka's Quinze armoire,
The other's stashed in Bannon's bar
    Together with both bollocks.

Or are they passed from hand to hand
    Like the Graeae's eye and tooth?
McGahn, McMaster, Mnuchin, Priebus:
Who will string the raddled rebus
    Of Trump's addled truth?

FASCIST OR PLUTOCRAT? *Harper's* demands;
    If your answer is "both," I'll cry *TOUché!*
His seething interior demons to calm
He lathers the masses and lards his own palm;
    I move that we dub him *Il Douché.*

For Trump our government is one
    Gargantuan selfie stick;
Likewise a Pantagruely grand
Prosthesis for his stumpy hand
    The public purse to pick.

Crooked, he cried, and swore to slap
    Her wrinkled wrists in fetters;
But just beneath each slam at her
Subtitles smirked, *An amateur!*
    I'd do it so much better!

Drain the swamp! That sucking sound
    His fans anticipated?
Porn-track for the phony czar
As Donald and his cronies are
    Financially fellated.

As contrapuntal bass, our base
    Administration offers
The gurgle, deep and leisurely,
As Donald drains the treasury
    Into confederate coffers.

Access Hollywood? Bush league.
    When all is said and done,
I'd shell out more for secret tapes
That might spell out the secret shapes
    Of *Access Washington.*

The lobbyists and hobnobists
    Don promised to embargo
Now find they simply can't refuse
To pay two hundred grand, plus dues,
    To schmooze at Mar-a-Lago.

As for that effluvial
      Potomac, dank and vasty—
After years of knocking it
He's resolutely stocking it
      With reptiles thrice as nasty.

As Chevron-Exxon mobilize
      Fresh derricks to erect,
And corporations swarm to get land,
Nice to know that there's *one* wetland
      Pruitt will protect.

That cabinet! A savvy set—
 For shifting, à la Pruitt,
The "P" in "E.P.A." to "Pillage"
Rates an A in Vice—no village
 Idiot could do it.

Description is defied by picks
 So sinister, so sorry;
But heck, I'll take a stab at it:
The Grand-Guignolest cabinet
 Since Dr. Caligari.

For each department's mission, a creep
　　Is shrewdly recruited to savage it;
And had we a veracious SPOX
She'd say, "Each henhouse gets the fox
　　Best qualified to ravage it."

In DeVostated schools, where coal
　　May fill in for Crayola,
Why fret if kids on Betsy's path
Flunk Reading, Writing, Science, Math?
　　They'll surely ace Payola.

Perry for Energy? There's a joke
　　We'll all enjoy the stink of:
The agency that, in debate,
Rick promised to eliminate
　　But somehow couldn't think of.

Interior? A jest that's ex-
　　Ponentially more stinky:
Teddy wannabe, Exxon shill,
Speaks loud and carries a big drill:
　　"Denyin' Ryan" Zinke.

Just like the Prez, the Sec of State
    Inspires each boy and goyl;
Each mother pipedreams: Will her son
Grow up to be, like Tillerson,
    A spout for Russian oil?

Boldly seeking strange and new
    Domains to screw the pooch in,
Trump gives D.C. what it desperately lacks:
More Treasury Secs from Goldman Sachs!
    Enter Steve Mnuchin—

Exit Czar, Foreclosure King,
    Ayatollah of homeowner terror,
Whose bank sought to bounce a nonagenarian
Dame from her digs for making a very in-
    Significant error—

Twenty-seven cents, to be exact—
    On a mortgage check she scribbled;
For while to his base Trump throws red meat,
His base he throws to the wolfish Street
    Like so much Costco kibble.

Not crowing, but elfin-slyly gloating,
    Jeff Sessions gets the goat
Of progressives who've upended
What the Founding Dads intended:
    One rich white man, one vote.

When to the sessions of Senate thought
    He summons up remembrance,
What never make it past the doors
Are powwows with ambassadors
    Of Slavic girth and cumbrance.

I could go on. But though their sins
     Be scarlet, or vermilion,
Those who serve at Donald's pleasure
Are superb by Donald's measure:
     They're worth a cool ten billion!

Cabinets, happily, soon break apart
     Like barstools smashed on stages;
But Trump's Supreme Court justice pick
Will haunt the poor, the weak, the sick
     For endless, friendless ages.

Though their two towers—ivy, gilded—
     May seem poles apart,
He who'd grudge all legal succor
To a fired and frozen trucker
     Shares Trump's frozen heart.

Yet the Prez, who scorns to rest
     Contented with the wrench
Justice gets from greed-glad Gorsuch
Is appointing dozens more such
     To the federal bench.

More such? No, not quite: for Gorsuch
    Knows, at least, his Wigmore;
As for others, let's acknowledge
That for basic legal knowledge
    One might trust a pig more.

Alt-right bloggers, Ku Klux snoggers,
    Homophobic bigots:
As Trump plumbs deep the fetid pool
His Senate (willing, swilling tool)
    Opens wide the spigots.

Ridiculous! Political!
    Disgraceful! Haters, too!
So-called judges!—so he's called
Our judges, and we stand appalled
    As his words come true.

Work with Congress? Too much like work.
    For the lazy, ukase is so sweet!
Negotiation's off the menu,
As is legislation, when you
    Mean to rule by tweet.

Come Auto! Come Pluto! Come Klepto and Krato!
    Come Oligo, Theo, Kakisto!
Come Ethno! Geronto! Nepo! Pseudologo!
Idioto! Agnoto! It's Prefix-a-Gogo!
    The -ocracy under whose fist (oh!)

We're squalidly squirming, we struggle to name,
    Our noggins increasingly numb:
Though fleetingly partial to *taurocoprocracy*,
My pleadings I'll marshall for *anticheirocracy*:
    To wit(ter), the Rule of Thumb.

Take (please!) his transgender ban:
    He plucked it from the ether—
Either that, or from his ass—
He didn't ask his seasoned brass
    And didn't tell them, neither.

Trans people, he claims, render our Forces
    Less potent, less lethal, less fearsome;
Yet in public-school restrooms (his policy states)
Trans teenagers must be repelled at the gates:
    It's perilous just to be near some!

Repeal Obamacare! he cried—
    The laws that bite, the clauses
That tax!—And yet what seemed a lark
Became the stalking of a Snark
    With comparable losses.

A brand-new Trump bestseller soon
    Will sweep a star-struck nation:
Art of the Fail: One Hundred Ways
To Pass, In Just One Hundred Days,
    No Major Legislation.

"Unfit," they keen—yet on the green
    He's surely fit, or fittish;
No *ifs*, no *ands*, no flaccid *buts*!
Behold the presidential putts!
    (Read it aloud, in Yiddish.)

Jeff Beauregard regards with joy
    A task that with glory rings:
Arm in arm with Pence and Kobach,
Mandate that America go back
    To Jim Crow's enfolding wings.

The Pence Election Commission's mission?
    Sins of omission. Each
State Secretary of State is urged:
Surrender your data, that we may purge
    Your voter rolls with bleach!

Or is it rather: one bot, one vote?
    Are all those data fated
To land in Fancy Bear's furry lap
So future votes can be (*clap, clap*)
    More handily invaded?

Either way, it gives one pause.
    Or should—and to their credit,
Forty-five states call Pence's bluff:
Refuse to send, or send their stuff
    After a pensive edit.

Stephen Miller, seed of migrants,
    Dracula-complected,
Drives stakes through Emma Lazarus
Lest sentiments so hazardous
    Be rashly resurrected.

Around the next stanza I'm building a fence
    (Or ring, like that of benzene),
Lest alien prosody pollute
My epic muse, compelling pursuit
    Of ruthless metric cleansing—

Trumpty Dumpty built a great wall;
Trumpty's Dummies paid for it all.
All the king's horseshit and all the king's men-
Dacity couldn't elect him again.

Resuming my stanza form (which I style
    The Fourteen-Wheeler, or Emilick),
I hasten to note that our border's still wall-less:
The G.O.P. Congress, though principally ball-less,
    For once forebears Donald's phlegm to lick.

Nor has Trump much better luck
    With his Not-A-Muslim-Ban:
When the order hits, its foes, fists clenched,
Hit the streets and airports, while at the bench
    The ordure hits the fan.

His lawyers strive repeatedly
    To make it look official;
But when your tweets, in essence, shout
LET'S KEEP THE DAMN SAND N*GG*RS OUT
    It's somewhat prejudicial.

Reader, I trust you won't recoil
        In shock, and want your cash back
If in our Donaldology
We stray from strict chronology
        And interpose a flashback.

Recall, if you can, that innocent Age
        Of moguls, nymphs, and satyrs
(Halcyon? Golden? Take your pick)
When dear old Don was just a *dic-*
        Not yet aspiring to *-tator.*

Of many satyrs ripe for satire
        In that goaty, gouty bazaar,
One whose hairy tale's worth telling
Is Felix, who preferred the spelling
        S-A-T-E-R.

Or: S-A-T-*T*-E-R—
        For oft this would-be Mellon
Would borrow, beg, or rent a T
To hide his true identity
        As twice-convicted felon.

Promising son of the Brighton Beach mob,
  He first manifested the seed of class
When, in a midtown watering-place,
He rather ingeniously slashed a foe's face
  With the stem of a smashed margarita glass.

From agg. assault to securities fraud
  Is quite a commendable jump;
As is his ascent, in what seems like an hour,
To a nest in the cloud-nuzzling heights of Trump Tower
  As Senior Advisor to Trump.

In copping a plea to fraud, he'd become
  (Prepare to hear Trump gulp) a
Faithfully fickle federal informant;
Rendering his racket, though not quite dormant,
  A sort of *felix culpa*.

Have I mentioned that Felix grew up with the once
  And future Michael Cohen, Esq.?
Have I named Mike's Ukrainian business ties, too?
(Have I asked myself why I'm I asking you
  When I simply could check my own text?)

With all the partners and porn stars he'd screwed
    And all the dough he was owin'
Don needed a pit bull with briefcase and phone,
And if dogcatcher Death had claimed his Cohn
    He'd settle for a Cohen.

Book One looked at some of Trump's mafia ties,
    From Atlantic City to Flushing;
A flaw in our jury-rigged, jerrycan job:
In loyalty to the American mob
    We might have slighted the Russian.

Cast your mind back to Chapter Eleven—
    Not of the poem: of the Code.
When toppling casinos left Trump in a bind,
Cohen and Sater helped Father Don find
    Mother Russia's motherlode.

If of legitimate lenders you took
    A statistically valid, quite large poll,
You'd find nearly all of them, having been shafted,
Or seen their competitors reamed, fore-and-afted,
    Wouldn't touch Trump with a bargepole.

Each dawn would greet beneath Trump's feet
    Some yawning Debt Valley to fill;
And if legitimate capital
He found he couldn't tap at all
    He'd happily tap the il-.

For haply, Donald's lack of cash
　　Was matched by his lack of scruples;
His multimillion-dollar flats
Were oleaginous laundromats
　　For oligarchic rubles.

Flats? In Soho, Trump Tower in toto
　　Was sheathed in mobsters' gilt.
Khomeinian brass ran money through
A Trump Hotel in far Baku
　　That squats there, still, half-built.

A seep—a drool—an ooze—soon
　　Swelled into a gusher,
Rarely flagging, of Poohtin-Bear honey:
Whence Junior's brag—"A lot of money
　　Pouring in from Russia."

Did Poohtin Bear himself take note?
　　His spooks did, double-quick:
Spying, *in re* Trump, the angle
That by dint of karats dangled
　　They might acquire a stick.

Goldenest carrot, openly phallic:
    A Trump World Tower in Red Square.
Entranced, our Ass advanced his position
By mounting in Moscow his exhibition
    Of Terra's best derrières.

Business in Russia can be rough
    Unless you pay the Czar off;
Doughty Don, no whit bewildered,
Took as partner "Putin's Builder"—
    Aras Agalarov.

"Will Putin be my new best friend?"
    Trump twittered like a 'tween.
But Vlad, the coolest kid in class,
Played hard-to-get, and at Don's bash
    Was sensed but never seen.

And yet, like Danaë in her windowless tower
    Deprived of her lover so bold—
The Thunderer, Zeus—did Don somehow feel,
As the poet relates in the Dossier of Steele,
    Vlad's love in a Shower of Gold?

At the Ritz-Carlton, Don took the suite
    Barak and Michelle had once graced;
How high, pray, would that picture rate
As *kompromat,* if micturat-
    Ing pros their bed defaced?

If true—and mind, I don't say it is—
    I'd never be so bold—
Though Trump at least once, if not (like Keats) much,
Had traveled (in Vegas with Aras's clutch)
    In the realms of gold—

If true, I say, this story warns us
    Strictly to eschew
Likening Don to der Führer, for
Strikingly (Eva could tell you more)
    Adolf preferred Number Two.

The year, by the by, was Twenty Thirteen.
    Vlad hadn't long to wait.
Curiouser and curiouser:
In Moscow, not Manchuria, sir,
    He'd found his Candidate.

While the runners sped cross-country
	One in blue, one red,
Wraithy packs of trolls and gremlins
Slipped from leashes by the Kremlin
	Snapped at Clinton's Keds.

"No Clear Link" between Russia and Trump:
	Thus the *Times*, untimely spinning
As full and final exoneration
An F.B.I. investigation
	That in fact was just beginning.

In that fateful election, the *Times*'s discretion
	F*cked the electorate o'er.
Henceforth, Gray Lady, this apothegm clasp:
A journalist's reach should exceed his grasp,
	Or what's a Franklin Foer?

Or if discretion you choose over valor,
	Sulzberger-King, don't be a plonker
By treating a male's malefactions so lightly
While each time a female trips even slightly
	You eagerly stoop to conk her.

Voters *could* have been alerted, at least,
    To the vastness of Vlad's cyber-violence,
Had not that treasonous terrapin, Mitch—
McConnell, McFunnel of wealth to the rich—
    Extorted the government's silence.

But *Comey* knew. How did he show
    His law-and-order ardor?
To Putin's thumb upon the scale
He joined his own, in weighty mail,
    And pushed a little harder.

Integrity, integrity,
    Macomety's got lots!
Which, preening in the looking glass,
Brings such catastrophes to pass
    As make the angels plotz.

No bulldog-jaw tenacity
    Henceforward can, I fear,
Efface or nullify or nix
The blot upon this spotted dick's
    Cheka'd (*sic*) career.

But the point, if not the blot, is moot;
    He'll never get the chance.
As the probe gets close-to-home-ier
The Boss's brash, back-slap encomia
    Turn to back-stab rants.

The axing stinks of Watergate's
    Most sanguinary news day:
But that the Don's incontinent rage
Harries him, pell-mell, to stage
    His massacre on a Tuesday.

First time as tragedy, second as farce:
    So Marx remarked 18th Brumairily;
So Donald confirms when he claims that the head
Of Comey must roll 'cause that heel of a Fed
    Had treated poor Hillary unfairily.

Like guilt-beclouded Claudius
    Unnerved by Hamlet's antics,
Trump trusts his Comecidal plans
To Rosenstein and Sessionkranz,
    A pair of sycophantics—

Apparently—for neither gives
     A damnlet for appearance—
Rosenstein's straight arrow's bent
While Sessionkranz's recusal's spent
     In venal interference.

But hold! Another shoe has dropped,
     Stiletto heel serrated:
Unfrocked, Doc Frankenstein may still
Be granted time to stalk and kill
     The victor he created!

Braving the orange minotaur's maze
     Jim left a paper trail;
Half man, half bullshit the monster looms
But Comey's meticulous memoing dooms
     His bovine covin to fail.

Those labyrinthine twists and turns—
     Dense as Ivanka's lokshen
Kugel—must, viewed from the bar
Of justice, show just what they are:
     A pattern of obstruction.

It's a hard rain that falls, so hard and fast
    That a person might plausibly posit
An errant Manila-based B-52
Was air-dropping every available shoe
    In chic Mrs. Marcos's closet.

It's hard to keep the sequence straight—
    To sort them, as Imelda would;
Forgive anachronism as
I strive to give the tale pizzazz
    As dear old Scott and Zelda would.

The day that Comey is cashiered,
    Rebuked, and sternly censured,
Trump ushers a jovial Russian pair
Into the Oval Office, where
    Few spooks have ever ventured.

No cod-roe spy, this Kislyak,
    But Beluga-grade, like Karla;
And yet this globular, bouncy boy
Inspires in Donald fiercer joy
    Than Ivana, Melania, or Marla.

When meeting with close allies, the Prez
    Clearly can't wait till it's over;
Yet here, embowered for an hour
With knakers of a hostile power—
    All smiles and *nazdarovya*.

How do we know? From photos that glowed
    In *Pravda* and *Izvestia;*
For the Russian press, with cameras and mikes
(And bugs, mayhap) were invited, but yikes—
    Not the Yanks—they're so much pestier!

I get the best intel, he crowed,
    And quite unprompted, shouted
Code-name details of an ISIS plot
In such profusion it promptly got
    A Mossad agent outed

And shut the golden spigots of
    Our allies' secret sources.
What a relief to know our Chief
Would never be a risk to brief
    As Hillary, of course, is.

He said he'd make the government
	Efficient, and he's done it;
Rather than make the Russians deal
With all the hassle of hacking, he'll
	Just open his mouth and run it.

To all the excuses his stooges and shills
	Have proffered, I'll offer one more:
In dealing with intelligence
Trump merits our indulligence—
	He's never had any before.

Out of the frying pan, into the trash fire:
	Such is the Donald's declension
When Rosenstein names, for his lamed repute's sake,
A Special Counsel whose spine's thrice as straight
	As a cable at maximum tension.

His rash cashiering the Donald now rues
	And his diaper grows palpably fuller;
For Comey, though twenty or thirty feet tall,
Really seems, to be fair, barely scary at all
	Next to the Stone Guest, Bob Mueller.

While Mueller methodically mulls the means
    Of prodding some pigeon to sing
(Subpoenas? Immunity? Threats or treats?)
Donald Junior obligingly tweets
    Two-thirds of Wagner's *Ring*.

Tying him to the Kremlin is
    A thread—a hawser, rather—
Of emails offering a fat
File of Clinton *kompromat*
    "Useful to your father."

 "If it's what you say I love it," gushed Don
    And hastened to implore
Kushner's and Manafort's inclusion
In a cold collation of collusion
    On the twenty-fifth floor.

In fairness, they'd good reason
    With treason thus to flirt:
When Natalya Vesel*nit*skaya
Pulls up a chair and sits by ya
    You know she's got the dirt.

Brooding one floor above: our epic's
    Feces-flinging hero.
Could Little White Hunter, then, forbear
To fetch Great Father these new-bagged bears?
    The odds, per Bannon: zero.

The topic, we're told, was "adoption"— adepts
    Know that's Russian for "lifting of sanctions"—
A *quid pro quo*, a *hic* for hacked mail,
A boon for Vlad's droogs whose quid by the bale
    Each clean corporation and bank shuns.

(But wait: am I falling for Fake News fibs?
    Why *shouldn't* the theme be adoption?
You don't have to be Hannitesquely hysteric
To wonder if, pondering Donnie and Eric,
    Trump might not consider the option.)

A smoking gun? Republicans,
    Of flapping flag so proud,
Would happily (you know it, sir!)
Ignore a smoking howitzer.
    They'd need a mushroom cloud.

Had a previous President dripped one drop
　　Of Trump's torrential rain
Of graft, collusion, overreach—
You can bet the farm he'd have been impeached
　　Before you could say "Hussein."

The bottom line: not one of these fine
　　Greeting-card patriots cares
If fair Columbia's Putin's fief
So long as they get tax relief
　　For suffering billionaires.

While Russian flames rage, congressional hacks
    Hustle to put out the smoke.
Eighty-six the probe? Let's give the part
To Intelligence's Maxwell Smart
    And the House's running joke.

Don't look here! Look there, at the Democrats'
    Smoking cigarettes!
A ploy whose point, despite the fewness
Of his frontal-lobe neurons, Devin Nunes
    Evidently gets.

Hey, Max—I mean Devin—next time you need
    Some specious secrets to leak,
Check out Pruitt's new appliance:
The forty-three-grand Cone of Silence
    Bespoke-made for a sneak!

In Washington, though, it seems Control
    Has given way to Chaos.
Whoever hasn't quit under a cloud
Has, for speaking sense too loud,
    Been elbowed off of the dais.

"Idiot." "Dope." "Dumb as sh*t."
*   "He sucks up and sh*ts down."*
"F*cking moron"—in this wise
The Chief is hailed by his own guys
    In Donald's Crazytown.

(Yet likening him to a grade-school kid,
    Per Mattis, is a ruddy
Slap to kids of any class,
Each of whom has had to pass
    A test in Social Studies.)

All the adults have left the room.
    No child-proof gates or locks.
Supervision's cursory
For a West Wing nursery
    With nukes instead of blocks.

Trump's Uncle Sam is Mr. Hyde
    Where once Sam seemed Doc Jekyll;
America's moral capital he
Has squandered far more rapidly
    Than all his father's shekels.

(*Update:* We knew the Great Performer
     Underperformed the Dow;
Now we know Fred's tax-fraudulent heir
Was a silver-spoon-fed half-billionaire
     Who from silk purse sewed ear of sow.)

Fond hopes reposed in Jaravanka's
     Cotillion-liberal words
Go up in carbon-laden fumes
As Dad, doyen of smoke-filled rooms,
     Torches the Paris Accord.

The concept of deterrence seems
     To baffle and confuse him;
With strategists he has a tiff:
*What's the point of H-bombs if
     We're not allowed to use 'em?*

Trump vows relentlessly to rain
     Death and devastation
On Pyongyang's Cities of the Plain;
Meanwhile, Fire, Fear, and Fury reign
     In his Administration.

In Charlottesville did Ku Klux Klan
    A stately march decree;
And when that hateful river ran
Into a crowd of friends of man,
    Murder, first degree

Ensued. Enthused by the Challenger
    That Heather couldn't dodge,
Trump challenges the party line:
The blame for mayhem, he opines,
    "On many sides" must lodge.

Swayed by the better angels (or lesser
    Devils) of his White House,
He rights himself, but then backslides:
"Some very fine people on both sides,"
    Says Trump, our moral lighthouse.

Rows of beaus with close-cropped hair,
    Ash castles in the air:
He's looked at Nazis from both sides now,
From good and bad, and still somehow
    Trump only seems aware

Of one blunt fact: They vote for him.
     They are his blood-sworn coven.
He loves to hear their black boots thump.
So what if they would gladly dump
     His grandkids in the oven?

The H-word is routinely ruled,
     By pedants, out of order;
Yet Trump himself has spilled the beans
By voicing, *re* the Philippines,
     His fondness for mass murder.

Hitler's speeches (Ivana teaches)
     Dwelt by Trump's bed in his palace:
Rarely read, one trusts, for he rarely reads:
But did its fearsome presence feed
     His manhood, like Cialis?

When Puerto Rico's smashed by storm
     Compassion melts his bowels;
Upon the blighted littoral, he
Dispenses Bounty literally
     By tossing paper towels.

Just sixty deaths, Trump still insists!
  His mathematic's nifty:
The value of a life that's brown
To one that's white, savants have found,
  Is roughly one to fifty.

Brown *dollars*, though—Donald & Co.
  Don't think *those* too dun or inky:
The thirty-mil grid-repair gig (see: *graft)*
Is snagged by a firm with a two-man staff
  Owned by a pal of Zinke.

As White House staffers lawyer up
    More lawyers undergird 'em;
Attorneys have attorneys who
Need counsel even more white shoe
    And so on ad absurdum.

All Hallows' Eve draws nigh! But why
    Does such abject afrightment
Seize in its talons the West Wing?
The breaking dawn, they know, will bring
    Mueller's first indictments.

Les jeux sont faits! The checkered wheel,
    Like spindle of the Fates,
Whirls, spun by unseen hands;
The sphere skips here, skips there, and lands—
    On Manafort and Gates.

Manafort! whose manifest
    Stratagem, it seems,
Is to shill for every tin-pot despot
And skim from every tin-pot's cesspit
    Pecuniary cream.

Manafort! whose manifold
    Transgressions and infractions
Should let Bob Mueller bring to bear
Upon yon short and curly hairs
    Considerable traction.

But if Bob's grip on Paul gives all
    Staunch liberals a hard-on,
Does the dream they're wanking on
Ignore the boon Paul's banking on:
    A presidential pardon?

Peace! Our poker-faced counsel keeps,
    Up his starched sleeve, some tricks:
Paving his federal case, you see,
He's saving New York State's A.G.
    A palletful of bricks.

A New York jury (some pal should tell Paul)
    Is unlikely to be hung;
And when, resounding ringingly,
The door swings shut in Sing Sing, he
    May wish that he had sung.

(Unless, in truth, he's soothed by the sound
     Of so secure a lock:
For who could subject to derision
Paul's preference for life in prison
     To death by Novichok?)

The god whose condign thunderbolts
     We conjured in the fall
Abjectly laid his missiles down;
But now an avatar is found
     Equipped to hurl them all.

In Bob we trust. We watch and wait.
     Though few and far between
(*Flynn! Papadopoulos! Manafort! Gates!*)
Each lightning flash illuminates
     A wider, wilder scene.

As if by searchlight lit, we glimpse
     The object of his searching:
A vast Collusionopolis
In which poor Papadopoulos
     Is just one squirming urchin.

Flynn flipped. George jumped. We watch and wonder,
   As each one takes Bob's bait,
How many defections Don *can* afford:
Though Paul may staunchly man a fort
   Will Rick throw wide the gates?

In mudslide ovations, Republicans crushed
    The fact they craved to forget:
That in lizard-brain lust for power and pelf,
Putting country fourth behind self, self, and self,
    The Party of Lincoln had set

(While Abraham gyred in his widening grave
    And pundits mea culpa'd)
On the bully pulpit a pitiful bully
Who'd not only stain and soil and sully
    The Constitution, but pulp it.

The State of the Union: Unhelmed, unhinged,
    Uncannily twisted and dented,
Untethered, unmoored, unhorsed, unmanned,
Un-Onioned (because a self-parody) and,
    In a word: *Unpresidented.*

We have no leader. A Leader (big L!)
    Is what we have instead:
Volodya's Useful Idiot
(How horrorshow to viddy it)
    And our own extruded Id.

Though his Sermon on the Hill may thrill
    The shills that fill the seats,
No teleprompted fleece can hide
The wolf that raveneth inside:
    Ye shall know him by his tweets.

Trump is the drunk at the end of the bar
     Muttering dark imprecations;
What once was your local, your great good place
Now wears a strange and sinister face;
     You're an alien in your own nation.

From the shadows down by the end of the bar
     Come laughter, catcalls, hooting;
The pub where everyone knew your face
Now feels like the sort of place
     The news shows in a shooting.

His Wall unbuilt, Trump finds new ways
    For wogs to be obstructed.
Let black and brown folks understand:
Cross this line drawn in the sand
    And your kids will be abducted.

Though the moral chops of a border cop
    Must not be over-nice,
Those eyes bewildered, dark and damp
In Kiddie Koncentration Kamps
    Should melt a heart of ICE.

Court-ordered to reknit kith with kin,
    Trump finds a kinder option:
Deport the parents, lose the files,
And watch kids' tears give way to smiles
    As they're offered for adoption!

Sexagenarian sexcapades
    (When not my own) quite bore me;
Yet duty bids me skim, at least,
The torrid tales of the *artiste*
    Whose *nom de con* is Stormy.

To be spanked with his phiz on a rolled-up Forbes
    Was Don's fondest dream come to pass;
For try as he might to contort like a toroid
He'd never quite mastered the trick ouroboroid
    Of kissing his own ass.

We titter, and tuck the tabloid back
    In its basket by the potty.
What Nostradamus dares prognose
That *poseur* Don might be deposed
    (In three senses) by M. Avenatti?

Many and many a hundred grand
    Changed hands before November
To hide from evangelicals
The sinfully stretched pellicule
    Of Donald's errant member.

SCREWING PORN STARS—no such phrase
    Will grace a federal docket:
But SCREWING WITH CAMPAIGN FINANCE.
The peccant part's not in his pants
    But in his jacket pocket.

Speaking of peccant parts, one Pecker—
    Prince of American Media—
Picked a peck of peccadilloes
From his pal's loquacious pillows
    (See *Catchandkillopedia*).

Paying off Pecker and playmates galore
    Was Fixer Mike, and it's comical:
Given the tab for Trump's fifth limb,
Taking Don to the vet and fixing *him*
    Might have been more economical.

But on wiles of masterminds like Mike
    What right have I to opine?
As Donald's prospects turned presidential
Essential Consultants proved essential
    To Cohen's bottom line.

As in its fecund Petri dish
    Frolics the protozoan,
So in his lush, secluded slush fund
(Sus fund? Rus fund? Tush fund? Hush fund?
    Crushin' it fund?) sloshed Cohen.

Korea Aerospace Industries,
    AT&T, Novartis,
And Viktor Vekselberg (Vlad's old buddy)
Kept the medium rich and muddy:
    Graft is where the heart is.

Don had no inkling (he claimed, unblinking)
    Of his fixer's capers and scrapes.
But wait!—to quote that hit Top Forty
Soon to be waxed by Berry Gordy:
    "Lordy, There Are Tapes!"

Beneath its crust of Cheeto dust
    Don's brow is damply glistening:
The bro who swore he'd take a slug for you
Hedged his bets and set a bug for you
    And now the Feds are listening.

Here comes the B-side! Not just tapes
    (Though those have left us reeling)
But gilt-edged Bible sworn upon:
I'm guilty, Your Honor—and so's the Don.
    The consigliere's squealing.

From courthouse corridors, north and south,
    The White House feels a raw gust.
The candles dance, the rafters moan—
Eight counts for Manafort, eight for Cohen:
    It's Hanukkah in August!

The dreidel spins its staggered path—
    Nomadic, vatic, fated—
Dervishes past you—past me—
And toppling, shows a great gilt "T"
    As Don is Trumplicated.

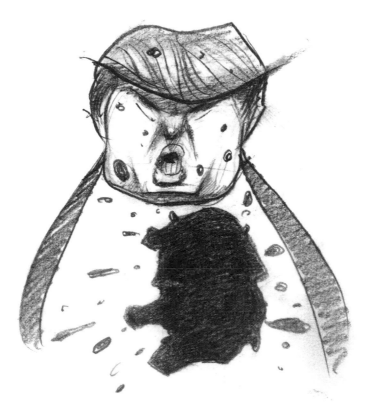

Having stalled one Supreme Court seat for a year
    And installed a stout plutocrat in it,
Our tortoise-shaped wrecking ball, stodgy and coy,
Makes sure Justice Kennedy's fateful fauteuil
    Is filled in a Louisville minute.

The President who would be King
    Ballooned above the Law
Taps the judge who seems the keenest
To protect him from subpoenas:
    Bart O'Kavanaugh.

It's fit that Brett should get a meta-
    Physical phylogeny:
If that venereal, vulpine codger
Roger Ailes had rogered Roger
    Stone, he'd be their progeny.

Clinton inquisitor? Torture booster?
    Foster conspiracy vendor?
Trafficker in purloined emails?
Ravisher of pure-loined females?
    Brawler on a bender?

As a rattling pack of skeletons
    Within his closet rages,
Republicans, with main and might,
Strain to keep the door shut tight
    On half a million pages.

Yet at the last hearing, the umpire's mask
    And cloak of dispassionate jurist
Are shed by Brett himself, revealing
White male privilege, squalling, squealing:
    Trumpery at its purest.

Falsus in omnibus—Kavanaugh's fibs
    Form a formidable list.
("Devil's Triangle"? Since you asked:
All three branches of government grasped
    In Donald's tiny fist.)

In wanton youth he drained and puked
    The volume of Lake Placid:
Pacific, civil hopheads fear
That Kavanaugh has done for beer
    What Manson did for acid.

You've come a long way, baby! The men who mocked
    Ms. Hill in the hearing room's glare
Now paternally pat Ms. Ford:
It isn't that we doubt your word;
    It's that we just don't care.

Even the Grand Pangrabb'em is coaxed
    To hold his contumelious tongue;
Until, in the glee of a rally, the cord
Grasped by his handlers snaps, and Ms. Ford
    On noose of derision is strung.

An elevator pitch provokes
    A game of Blind Man's Bluff:
McConnell and Grassley laugh themselves hoarse
As Trump sends Special Agents forth
    Blindfolded, gagged, and cuffed.

In days to come, when kibitzing
    The SCOTUS's debates,
On planes not-so-subliminal
We'll spell it out: *Sex Criminals*
    Of The United States.

Five thousand lies and counting, say
　　The checkers who detect 'em;
Pinocchio's nose has spanned the globe,
Cameled 'neath his tented robe
　　And burrowed in his rectum.

We once thought Trump's untruth a means
　　His mean ends to fulfill;
But now we know it is an end:
To make our mere reality bend
　　To his triumphant Will.

His followers know it, and willingly trade
　　The world for a globe of phlegm
Teeming with fables, phobias, fibs—
If it's false enough to enrage the Libs
　　It's true enough for them.

In the stable of confidence tricksters, Trump's truly
　　A genius. Come, let's not be reticent:
Inventing a way to make darkness from light
And turn our democracy's noon into night—
　　He must be a sort of con Edison!

Enemy of the People (though Fox
    And Friends he'd fain acquit):
So Donald styles the press; and Bannon
Well describes his answering cannon:
    "Flood the zone with sh*t."

Lest steaming turds fail to deter
    The press from doing their job,
Donald steals a second look
At his *Highly Effective Demagogues* book:
    "Step 2: Arouse the mob."

As word to the wise, Trump graciously lets
    Jared's pal's Gestapo
Dismember—sorry, *interrogate*—
A member of the Fourth Estate
    Who writes for Jeff Bezos's WaPo.

Recall Greg Gianforte, who full-body-slammed
    A journo for daring to question him?
Says Trump in Missoula: *Don't ever try
To wrestle him. Never. He's my kind of guy!*
    (Of course, rallies bring out the best in him.)

To judge by the timing, here's Trump's hidden text
    (Tell me if I've got the gist right):
The fifteen Saudis who valiantly fought
Khashoggi are Trump's kind of guys, for they brought
    A bone saw to a fistfight.

Borscht-belt tummler, demon trumpeter,
    He grimaces—inhales—
Then riffs and scats his blackshirt jazz,
Channeling with chill pizzazz
    White hate that never pales.

Mirrors, smoke, and sonorous
    Word-salading make certain
That each bewitched, befuddled fan
Pays no attention to the man
    Behind the Iron Curtain.

Meanwhile, the news keeps cycling, like
    A car alarm berserk:
Trade wars brewing! Climate stewing!
Migrants massing! Summer suing!
    Trump's thumbs hard at work!

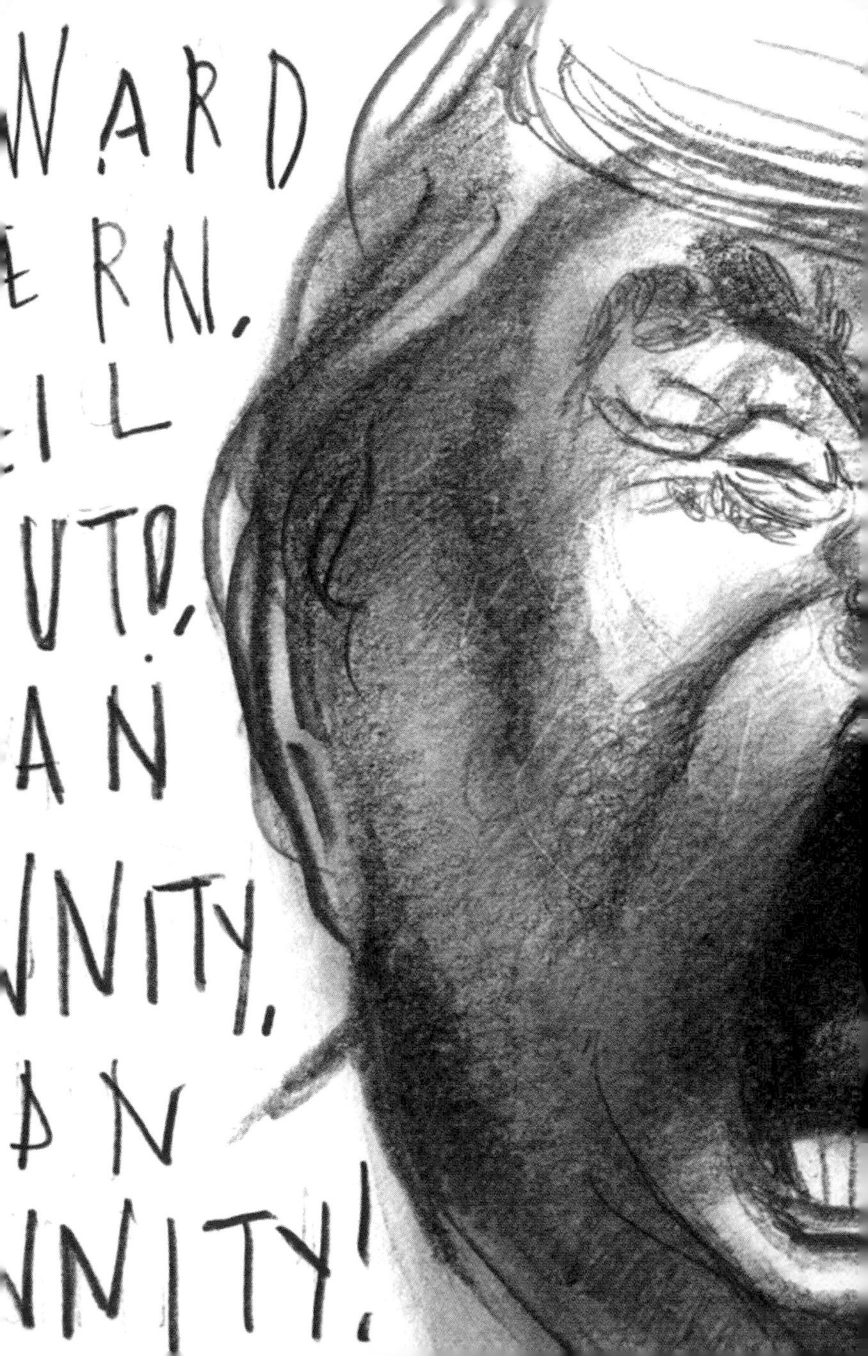
WARD
ERN,
IL
UTO,
AN
NITY,
AN
NITY!

After months of grilling, Paul's flipped at last
　　By Bob, our long-order cook;
Cries of *Witch Hunt!* can't draw the curtain
Now that Mueller knows for certain
　　In which broom closet to look.

The once revilèd Rocket Man
　　Trump now finds *ravissant*.
What beckons him to this kimchi'd bower?
Is it Kim's totalitarian power
　　Or his totally rad bouffant?

Trump's hothouse flowers of hate now bloom
　　In pipe bombs, assault rifles, pistols;
In disbelief we hear the din
In Pittsburgh now, as once Berlin,
　　Of screams and splintered crystal.

The question that perplexes me
　　As I assess the vague
But very nasty smell about:
Is Trump a salmonella bout
　　Or the bubonic plague?

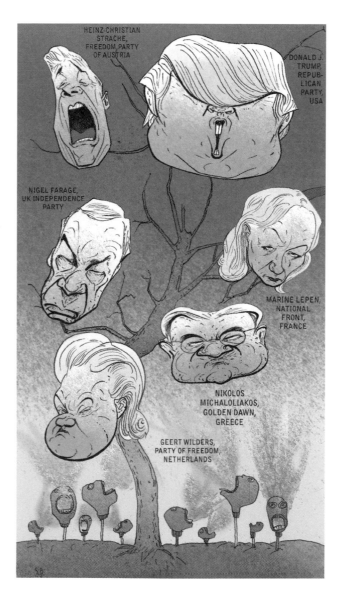

HEINZ-CHRISTIAN STRACHE, FREEDOM, PARTY OF AUSTRIA

DONALD J. TRUMP, REPUB-LICAN PARTY, USA

NIGEL FARAGE, UK INDEPENDENCE PARTY

MARINE LEPEN, NATIONAL FRONT, FRANCE

NIKOLOS MICHALOLIAKOS, GOLDEN DAWN, GREECE

GEERT WILDERS, PARTY OF FREEDOM, NETHERLANDS

A bug the body politic
    Will presently eject,
From this end or from that? Or is he
Part of a pandemic busy
    Vectoring, unchecked?

In Trump—in Brexit—in the *Resurrexit*
    Of parties of hatred and death—
In Cambridge Analytica—
We feel a wind mephitic, a
    Soupçon of Putin's borscht breath.

Russia, Turkey, Hungary,
    Poland, Brazil, Venezuela:
Does virulent autocracy
Mean liberal democracy
    Is doomed, so soon, to failure?

If Trump is just a fluke, a sport
    Spawned by the media jungle,
We'll just unseat him and move on.
But what if the succeeding Don
    Succeeds where this one bungled?

Even for *this* burlesque Caesar (Sid?)
    It's no foregone conclusion
We'll foil his grand Caligula bid;
Thus Book Two ends as Book One did:
    In hope—in dread—in confusion.

Checks and balances? Bounced and drained
    As plutocrats loot our heritage;
Only a Democratic House
Can save us from this insatiable Louse
    And these fleas of Newt's vile parentage.

Despite hopeful polls, those hackers and trolls
    Are mustering in my mind's eye;
For Vlad, who now we know *did* steal the last one,
Is hard at work pulling *another* fast one
    As Don, Paul, and Mitch turn a blind eye.

Meanwhile, Sessions and G.O.P. Secs
    Of State who manage the rolls
Make sure that every trap is sprung
To keep folks black, brown, red, and young
    From flexing their might at the polls—

Canting to forty degrees a field
    Already tilted to thirty
By dark money, gerrymandering, and
Oligarchic plans wherewith the hands
    Of the Founding Fathers were dirty.

They had the best intentions, of course:
    Preventing mob rule their priority.
But Alexander, you rapping fool—
In your long-running show we now *have* mob rule
    And oddly, the mob's a minority.

A warlike, unlettered, fanatical tribe
    Of desert, mountain, and plain—
With rich merchants allied—in this mythical land
(Let's call it—oh, I don't know—*Krizhtyanistan*)
    Of all sway has gathered the reins.

Machinery broken, the stage is set
    For a third act that some might find jocular:
A demagogue whose *demos* isn't agog,
But aghast; a prince kissed by Pepe the Frog;
    A populist deeply unpopular.

Holding his peace (unlike Jim!) in the wings,
    Bob Mueller stokes hope, even jollity;
But what if our lantern-jawed *deus ex machina*'s
Shackled and gagged before he can put back in a
    Semblance of order our polity?

Were my mouth as full of song as the sea,
    Had my tongue ten thousand asps' venom,
Had my notebook twenty trumpillion pages
I still couldn't chronicle all Don's outrages
    Or find enough aeons to pen 'em.

In White House or Big House, impeached or enthroned,
    The Donald's a theme without equal.
Though this poem's entombed now in tome, I'm inspired
To tap out more cantos. Muse, you're rehired!
    Let's get to work on the sequel!

ACKNOWLEDGMENTS

My thanks go, first of all, to my brilliant and generous collaborator, Steve Brodner; to my old friend David Rothenberg, who made this book happen; to Martin Pedanik, who made it handsome; to Marc Lowenthal of the MIT Press, for encouragement and guidance; and to my agent and friend of nearly four decades, Joe Spieler.

Friends, colleagues, and relatives too numerous to enumerate have offered support and advice. I am grateful to them all, but especially to Eva Barnett, Howard Berkowitz, Walter Blanco, Barry Blitt, Vicki Brower, Gerald Cohen, Larry Cohler-Esses, Brian Cullman, Melissa Easton, Barat Ellman, Elodie Ghedin, Jay Golan, Gershom Gorenberg, Michael Gottsegen, Hendrik Hertzberg, Robin Hirsch, Roald Hoffmann, Taylor van Horne, Marsha Howard, Phillip Johnston, Tobi Kahn, Star Lawrence, Adam Linson, Mitch Loch, Ramsey Margolis, Bodo Mrozek, Geoffrey O'Brien, Tim Page, Marcia Pally, Craig Pascal, Deborah Rosenthal, Dan Rothstein, Rich Scharaga, Leslie Schnur, Elliott Sharp, Mark Shulgasser, Michael Singer, Edward Sorel, Caroline Stern, Dirk Trauner, and Peter Wallach, and most especially to Henry Bean, Sharon Dolin, Howard Eisenberg, Stuart Klawans, Evan Parker, Jed Perl, Umru Rothenberg,

Ray Scheindlin, Victor Shargai, Dave Soldier, Rob Schwimmer, Alicia Svigals, and Rafi Zabor. I am grateful, as well, to Terra Nova's many Kickstarter supporters, a list that overlaps with this one and is growing as we go to press. Of my club-foot rhythms and imperfect rhymes, they are all perfectly blameless.

The *Trumpiad* is based (however louchely) on testimony, reporting, and analysis by hundreds of hard-working journalists, historians, social scientists, and public servants, among them Anne Applebaum, Wayne Barrett, Emily Bazelon, Ari Berman, Ian Bassin, John Brennan, James Comey, David Corn, Adam Davidson, John Dickerson, Kurt Eichenwald, David Farenthold, Ronan Farrow, Marc Fisher, Franklin Foer, Masha Gessen, D.D. Guttenplan, Luke Harding, Virginia Heffernan, Susan Hennessey, Seth Hettena, Michael Isikoff, David Cay Johnston, John Judis, Ezra Klein, Michael Kranish, Ivan Krastev, Steven Levitsky, Dahlia Lithwick, Josh Marshall, Jane Mayer, Greg Miller, Yascha Mounk, Robert Mueller, David Plotz, Jennifer Richeson, Timothy Snyder, Zephyr Teachout, Rebecca Traister, Craig Unger, Jacob Weisberg, Benjamin Wittes, Michael Wolff, Bob Woodward, and Daniel Ziblatt.

Finally, to my wife Freda and our daughter Sara Xing, my deepest gratitude and love.

—E.E.

November 2018

Evan Eisenberg's essays and satire have appeared in *The New Yorker*, *The Atlantic*, *The Nation*, *The New Republic*, *Time*, *Esquire*, and the *New York Times*. His book *The Ecology of Eden* has been hailed as "a prose epic [of] dazzling wit and impressive learning" (*Washington Post)* and a "tour de force of magnificent visionary sweep" (*Sunday Times*, London), while *The Recording Angel* has been selected as one of the "50 greatest music books ever" by the *Observer* (U.K.).

Widely credited with spearheading the revival of drawn satire over the past four decades, **Steve Brodner** has been a regular contributor to *The New Yorker*, *Rolling Stone*, the *New York Times*, *Harper's*, *Esquire*, *Playboy*, *Mother Jones*, *The Nation*, and the *Los Angeles Times*. Recipient of numerous awards, including the Hamilton King Award and the Aronson Award for Social Justice Journalism, Brodner has been hailed by Lewis Lapham as "a born arsonist" and by Edward Sorel as "incomparable… the best caricaturist around."